SUFFRAGETTE

LEVEL 3

SCHOLASTIC

Adapted by: Jane Rollason

Publisher: Jacquie Bloese

Designer: Annette Peppis

Picture research: Pupak Navabpour

Photo credits:
All film stills provided courtesy of Pathé Productions
Pages 5–7: Heritage Images/Getty Images.
Page 54: Hulton Archive/Getty Images.
Pages 58 & 59: Heritage Images, Popperfoto, Topical Press
Agency/Getty Images; March of Woman/Mary Evans Picture
Library.

Published by Scholastic Ltd. 2016

Mary Glasgow Magazines (Scholastic Ltd.)
Euston House
24 Eversholt Street
London NW1 IDB

Printed in Malaysia

Contents

	Page
Suffragette	**8–57**
People and places	**4–5**
The story so far	**6–7**
Chapter 1: Maud	8
Chapter 2: Violet	12
Chapter 3: Maggie	15
Chapter 4: Mr Lloyd George	20
Chapter 5: Sonny	26
Chapter 6: Mrs Pankhurst	33
Chapter 7: Mr Taylor	38
Chapter 8: Inspector Steed	41
Chapter 9: George	45
Chapter 10: Edith	49
Chapter 11: Emily	53
Fact File: The Suffragettes	**58–59**
Self-Study Activities	**60–63**
New Words	**64**

SUFFRAGETTE

SONNY WATTS

is Maud's husband. He also works at the laundry. He is a kind man. He and Maud have a young son, George.

MAUD WATTS

works at the Glass House Laundry in Bethnal Green in London. She has worked there since she was seven years old.

EMILY DAVISON

is a militant suffragette. She has been to prison many times.

NORMAN TAYLOR

owns the Glass House Laundry. He is not a nice man.

DAVID LLOYD GEORGE

is an important Member of Parliament (MP).

INSPECTOR STEED

is a police officer. His job is to watch the suffragettes. He believes in the law, even when the law is wrong.

EMMELINE PANKHURST

is the leader of the suffragette movement. She started the Women's Social and Political Union (WSPU) in 1903.

EDITH ELLYN

and her husband,

HUGH,

run a chemist's in Bethnal Green. Edith is middle class, studied at university and is a suffragette.

VIOLET MILLER

is another worker at the laundry. She has several children and is a suffragette.

ALICE HAUGHTON

is married to an MP. She is rich and knows many important people. She is a suffragette.

PLACES

BETHNAL GREEN
is in the East End of London. This was a poor part of the city, where working-class people lived and worked.

THE HOUSE OF COMMONS
is the home of the British Parliament, where MPs make the country's laws.

HOLLOWAY PRISON
is a women's prison in north London.

THE STORY SO FAR

This story takes place in London in 1912.

In 1912, men and women did not have the same rights. Fathers and husbands controlled women's lives. Women couldn't vote and they couldn't become Members of Parliament (MPs). They worked and they looked after Britain's homes and children, but they couldn't help to make the laws of the land. Politics was a man's world.

The campaign to win the vote for women had grown during the nineteenth century, and by 1900, many MPs believed that women should have the vote. But change was slow. The campaign was too polite, and not enough people were listening.

In 1903, Emmeline Pankhurst decided stronger action was needed. She started the Women's Social and Political Union (WSPU). Their slogan was 'Actions, not words' and the colours were purple, green and white. It had a militant programme.

In 1912, Mrs Pankhurst decided the campaign needed to be on the front page of the newspapers. And that's when our story starts.

What is a suffragette?

The word 'suffragette' comes from the noun 'suffrage', which means 'the right to vote'. Most British newspapers did not like Mrs Pankhurst and her new ideas. In 1906, one newspaper called these militant women 'suffragettes'. It was meant to be a joke, but the women liked the word and used it proudly.

CHAPTER 1
MAUD

The bell rang in the Glass House Laundry. Lines of women cleaned out big washing bowls and put down hot irons. Men turned off the machines. Maud dried her red hands, grateful that another day was over. She imagined the smiling face of her little boy, George, waiting for her when she got home.

But her day wasn't quite over.

'Take this up to the West End for me, Maud,' said Mr Taylor, throwing her a packet of laundry. Norman Taylor was the owner of the Glass House Laundry. 'They want those clean shirts by six o'clock.'

It was the men's job to take the clean laundry around London, but someone had forgotten this packet. Mr Taylor knew that Maud always did what he asked. Maud picked up the shirts and ran to catch a bus. Before long, the bright lights of the West End department stores came into view.

Maud got off the bus in Regent Street. It was busy with shoppers and office workers. Maud passed a rich lady in an expensive coat and an older woman carrying a baby, covered with a scarf. She noticed a woman reading a newspaper beside a news stand.

Then one of the shop windows caught Maud's attention. It showed a picture of a family on the beach. Maud had never seen the sea. She thought about going there with George and playing on the warm sand.

The woman with the baby passed her again, and looked quickly at the woman reading the newspaper. The big clock outside the department store moved towards six o'clock. Maud was about to leave when she heard voices shout out behind her.

'Votes for women! Votes for women!'

Suddenly, the shop window broke into a thousand pieces. Glass flew everywhere. The woman with the baby, the rich lady and the woman with the newspaper were all throwing stones. They shouted slogans and waved flags of purple, green and white, as screams filled the air.

Some people ran while others stood shocked, unable to move. Maud wanted to get away from the trouble, but she tripped and dropped her laundry. The packet opened and the clean, white shirts fell onto the dirty street. Maud cut her hand on a piece of broken glass as she picked them up.

Maud saw a bus moving slowly along the crowded road. She got on and looked back at the women. Among the faces was a woman who worked at the laundry. Her name was Violet Miller and she'd started work three weeks before. Violet noticed Maud too and smiled.

'Votes for women!' she shouted, throwing another stone at a department store window. Maud looked away quickly.

When she got home, Sonny was sitting by the fire, reading the newspaper. It was quiet and warm. Their son was in bed.

'Are you all right?' Sonny asked. 'You're late.'

'I had to take a parcel up to the West End for Taylor,' Maud said.

Sonny noticed the blood on her hand.

'You're hurt,' he said. 'What happened?'

'It's nothing,' said Maud. 'There was some trouble on Regent Street. It was those women – the suffragettes. They broke all the shop windows.'

'Trouble makers,' said Sonny. 'They're getting worse.'

'I know,' said Maud. 'It was terrible.'

She didn't say anything about Violet to Sonny.

'I'll take that packet for you in the morning,' Sonny said. 'Are you coming to bed?'

'I'm just going to wash the shirts again,' Maud said.

She put some water over the fire to heat and placed the dirty shirts into a big bowl. One more job before she could sleep.

＊＊＊

Early the next morning, Maud opened her eyes to another day. Her life was hard and she was always tired. She played with George while she dressed him, and then made breakfast for everyone. After leaving George with her neighbour Mrs Garston, she passed a boy selling newspapers.

'Suffragettes attack London shops: Mrs Pankhurst disappears!' he shouted.

'They're mad,' thought Maud, as she hurried to work.

CHAPTER 2

VIOLET

The women were already doing the first wash when Violet arrived. She hurried to her place among them, but Mr Taylor had seen her.

'Oi!' he shouted. 'Mrs Miller!' He came over to speak to her. 'You're late again.'

'Sorry, Mr Taylor,' said Violet. 'It's only a few minutes.'

'That's the second time you've been late,' he said, 'and you've only been here three weeks. Don't you want this job, Mrs Miller?'

There was a mean smile on his face.

'Yes,' said Violet quickly. 'I won't be late again, I promise.'

Maud was watching them. 'Mr Taylor,' she shouted. 'There's a problem with my machine.'

Mr Taylor's smile disappeared. 'All the machines were checked on Friday,' he said.

'Well, I can smell burning from this one,' said Maud.

As Mr Taylor called one of the men over, Maud looked across at Violet. Both women smiled.

Later that morning, Violet was ironing next to Maud.

'Thanks for earlier,' Violet whispered. She moved closer to Maud. 'If you're interested, we meet on Mondays and Thursdays. At Ellyn's, the chemist's. Mrs Ellyn leads the East End group.'

***

It was the end of the day and the women were taking off their wet clothes. The air in the laundry was always hot and wet, and several of the women were coughing.

Many had burns on their arms and hands. Violet was with a young girl of about twelve years old.

'This is Maggie, my eldest,' Violet said.

'Hello, Maggie,' said Maud, with a friendly smile.

Outside the laundry, they saw a small crowd by the gates. A woman was standing on a step, speaking to the laundry workers.

'It's Mrs Haughton,' Maud told Violet. 'She's the MP's wife.'

'In this country, the law gives men all the rights over our children, our money and our homes,' Alice Haughton was saying. 'We women have no rights.'

Men at the edge of the crowd jeered and made jokes but Alice paid no attention to them.

'But there is hope for the future,' she said to the women. 'The Prime Minister wants to hear from working women around the country. He has asked us to come to Parliament. We work like men. We should have the vote like men!'

'You've never worked in your life!' shouted one of the men, laughing rudely.

'I want one woman from this laundry to speak at the House of Commons,' Alice continued. 'The MP Mr Lloyd George will listen to you!'

'No one cares, love,' shouted Mrs Coleman, an older laundry worker.

'Some of us do, Mrs Coleman,' said Violet, 'so you can just shut up!'

Everyone laughed again.

'Thank you for listening,' said Alice. 'Votes for women!'

Violet turned to Maud. 'Are you going to speak for us laundry girls?' she asked.

'Mr Taylor's a good employer,' said Maud.

'To you, maybe,' said Violet.

Maud looked at her sharply. 'You've only been here three weeks,' she said. 'You don't know anything.'

They began to walk home. Violet's other children ran ahead of her, laughing and playing. Violet watched them.

'I started in a laundry when I was thirteen,' she said. 'Maggie's only twelve, and she's in here already. We've got to fight to get a better life.'

Maud looked at Violet. 'By breaking windows?' she said. 'It's not right.'

And she turned off the main road towards her home.

CHAPTER 3

MAGGIE

Maud and Sonny sat with George at the table. It was nearly George's bedtime, and Sonny was doing a trick for him. Sonny put his hand over a pile of three coins. He moved his hands quickly and the coins were gone. They were in his other hand. George laughed.

The coins were part of Sonny's pay for the week.

'Have you got yours?' Sonny asked Maud. Maud pulled out a small brown packet from her pocket. Sonny opened it and counted out the coins, putting them in a pile next to his.

'Mummy hasn't got as many coins as you,' said George.

Sonny laughed and looked at Maud.

'That's just how it is,' he said. 'It's always been that way.'

Sonny did the trick again with Maud's money. George's laugh was turning into a cough. Maud put her arm around him.

'Did you see Mrs Haughton outside the laundry this evening?' she asked Sonny. 'She thinks women should get the same money as men.'

'She doesn't know anything about working in a laundry,' said Sonny. 'I could do your job but you couldn't do mine.' He picked up their son. 'Come on, George. Say goodnight to the King and then it's bedtime.'

Sonny held George up in front of a picture of King George V on the wall.

'Good night, sir,' said George.

'Good boy,' said Sonny.

George started to cough again.

Maud looked worried. 'I'm taking him to the chemist's after work tomorrow,' she said.

***

While Edith Ellyn, the chemist, was listening to George's chest, Maud looked around the shop. On the wall there was a photograph of Mrs Pankhurst, the leader of the suffragettes.

'Are you a suffragette, Mrs Ellyn?' Maud asked.

'Yes,' said Edith. 'We women are at war against the men who run this country, Mrs Watts.'

'And what about the women who are going to speak to Mr Lloyd George?' Maud asked. 'Will that make a difference?'

'I don't know,' said Edith. 'It's actions not words that will get us the vote.'

Edith turned back to George. 'You'll be fine, young man,' she said. 'Would you like a sweet?'

The shop bell rang and an older woman came in. Maud knew her face. She had seen her that day in Regent Street, carrying what she thought was a baby. But there had been no baby, only a bag of stones.

'Good afternoon,' said the woman. 'Are the others here?'

'Not yet, Miss Withers,' said Edith. 'But please go through to the back room.'

Edith gave Maud a small bottle of medicine. 'One spoonful each morning and evening,' she explained.

Maud got out her purse.

'No, no,' said Edith. 'There's nothing to pay.'

Maud thanked Edith and her husband, Hugh, who was mixing up medicines on the other side of the shop.

Outside, Maud bent down to do up George's coat. She didn't see the camera that was pointing at her, a few metres away. She didn't notice the sound as it took a photograph. Another woman arrived at Ellyn's for the meeting, and the camera took another photo.

✶✶✶

The next day, Inspector Arthur Steed called a meeting at Bethnal Green police station. He invited other police officers and two Members of Parliament, including Benedict Haughton, Alice Haughton's husband.

Inspector Steed showed them some photographs of women outside Ellyn's, the chemist's.

'These were taken two days ago,' he explained. 'Let's start with Edith Ellyn. She's clever. We've arrested her nine times, and she's been to prison four times. She has studied at university and has no children – she's dangerous. And this is her husband, Hugh Ellyn. He owns the chemist's. If he was a woman, he'd be a suffragette!'

The men laughed. The inspector moved on to a photograph of Violet Miller.

'Violet's an old hand,' he said. 'She moves around a lot. We've arrested her several times and she's been to prison twice. A new baby comes along every nine months. Her husband drinks all their money and hits her for fun.'

Mr Haughton picked up a photograph of Maud.

'And who's this?' he asked.

'That's Maud Watts,' said Inspector Steed. 'A new one. We haven't seen her before.'

✶✶✶

Maud was hurrying to Mr Taylor's office with a pile of paperwork. She opened the office door without knocking and went in. When she saw her employer, her papers fell to the floor. He was there with Maggie, Violet's daughter, his hand under her skirt as he tried to kiss her. Maggie was crying and doing her best to push him away.

When he saw Maud, Mr Taylor stopped. Maud turned and ran to a dark corner of the factory. She needed to be alone. Covering her face with her hands, she remembered all the times it had happened to her. She had been twelve when it started, just like Maggie.

Later, Mr Taylor came over while Maud was drying some clothes.

'What did you want before, Maud?' he said.

'We're … we're short of soap for the big machines,' Maud said. She was still feeling sick inside.

'Don't come to me with that,' said Mr Taylor. 'Go to Derek, in the buying office.'

And then he spoke quietly into her ear. 'She's just like you at that age,' he said. He was smiling, but his eyes were angry.

At the end of the day, Mr Taylor called across the laundry to Violet.

'People tell me you're going to speak at the House of Commons, Mrs Miller,' he said.

The men around him laughed.

'Yes, tomorrow,' said Violet. 'I've already worked the extra hours. I worked late Tuesday and Thursday.'

'Leave the vote to us, Mrs Miller,' said Mr Taylor, 'and we'll leave the housework to you!'

Maud watched the men laughing. She was tired of it.

'Violet!' she shouted. 'I'll come with you.'

Now the men started to jeer at Maud.

Sonny came up to Maud. He wasn't like the other men, but he didn't like being laughed at.

'Maud, what are you doing?' he said.
'I'm just going to listen,' Maud told him.

CHAPTER 4

MR LLOYD GEORGE

The next day, groups of women walked towards the House of Commons, many carrying flags with the name of their home town. Maud felt small next to the government buildings, as she looked around for Violet and Alice Haughton.

She caught sight of Violet and waved. Her smile disappeared, however, when she got closer and saw Violet's face. It was black and blue.

'Oh, Violet!' said Maud. 'Did your husband do that?'

'It's nothing,' said Violet. 'I'm all right.'

Violet was walking with difficulty, and she took Maud's arm. Together they went into the House of Commons, where they met Alice Haughton.

Alice looked at Violet's face. 'Oh, my dear ... ,' she said.

'Glass House Laundry next,' called a voice across the hall. 'Then Hackney Piano Makers, straight after.'

'I'm fine,' said Violet.

'You're not fine, Violet,' said Alice. 'You can't go in front of Lloyd George like this.'

'Glass House Laundry,' the voice called again.

'You speak for me, Maud,' said Violet.

'Oh, no,' said Maud. 'I can't.'

Maud tried to walk away, but Alice held on to her.

'You can do it, Maud,' she said.

'There must be someone else,' said Maud. 'I don't know what to say.'

'Glass House Laundry, please!' The voice was becoming impatient.

'There's no time to find anyone else,' said Alice, leading Maud towards the room where the MPs were waiting.

David Lloyd George sat behind a large table with other MPs on either side of him. The room was full. Violet and Alice found seats at the back.

The room fell silent as Maud walked between the rows of men. She sat at a small table in the centre of the room, and a woman began typing on a machine. Maud's heart was racing.

'Mrs Miller,' said Mr Lloyd George. 'Please begin.'

'It's Watts, sir,' said Maud. 'Mrs Watts. Mrs Miller isn't able to speak.'

'Do you also work at the Glass House Laundry in Bethnal Green, Mrs Watts?' he asked.

'Yes, sir, I was born in the laundry.'

'Then tell us about your life there.'

'I don't know what to say.' Maud looked down at her hands.

Mr Lloyd George gave her a kind smile. 'Did your mother work at the laundry?'

'From when she was fourteen, sir,' said Maud. 'She took me with her. I slept in a corner, while she worked. All the women did it.'

'The owner of the laundry allowed that?'

'Mr Taylor wants the women back as soon as possible after having their babies,' she said.

'And does your mother still work at the laundry?' asked Mr Lloyd George.

'She died when I was four,' said Maud. 'There was an accident with hot water.'

The room went silent.

'And your father?' asked Mr Lloyd George.

'I never knew him, sir,' she said.

'So you work for Mr Taylor now?' he said.

'Yes, part time from when I was seven, with a bit of school, then full time from twelve,' said Maud. 'I was good at the work. I became head washer at seventeen, and now I manage the girls. I'm twenty-four, so...'

'You're very young to have that position,' said Mr Lloyd George.

'It's a short life in the laundry for a woman,' said Maud. 'You'll probably get a cough from the chemicals. You might lose your fingers in the machines. You get burns, headaches ...'

'And how much do you earn?' Mr Lloyd George asked.

'We get thirteen shillings* a week, sir. We work a third

* In old British money, there were 20 shillings in one pound.

more hours than the men, and they get nineteen shillings a week. And they're outside most of the time, so they're in the fresh air.'

'Why do you want the vote, Mrs Watts?' he asked.

Maud thought for a moment. 'Maybe our lives don't have to be like this. Maybe they can be better. '

Everyone was quiet.

'Thank you, Mrs Watts.' There were tears in Mr Lloyd George's eyes. 'The government will decide soon. Words like yours may change opinions.'

∗∗∗

It was late when Maud got into bed next to Sonny. She told him all about her adventure at the House of Commons.

'I can smell drink on you,' he said.

'I've only had a glass of wine,' said Maud. 'Mrs Haughton bought it.'

'Are you a suffragette now, Maud?' Sonny sounded worried.

'No,' said Maud. She turned onto her side away from him.

'You know how the boys at work laugh at Violet,' said Sonny. 'They'll laugh at you too.' He held her close. 'I'm only trying to protect you, Maud,' he said. 'Like I always do.'

'I know,' she said.   ∗∗∗

After work the next day, Maud received an invitation to tea from Edith Ellyn.

'You've woken up the old men of Westminster*,'

* The government offices are in Westminster, so Edith is talking about the government.

laughed Edith, hanging up Maud's coat. While Edith was making tea, Maud looked around at all the bottles of medicine.

'So your husband knows about all these chemicals?' she asked.

'No.' Edith smiled. 'This is his business, but he doesn't understand the chemistry. I'm the chemist.'

'How long have you been married?' asked Maud.

'Twenty-three years now,' said Edith. 'I wanted the business to become "Ellyn and Daughters", but we never had any children.' Then she changed the subject. 'Alice told me you spoke well yesterday.'

'I was so nervous,' Maud said, and she started to tell Edith all about her big day.

***

When Maud got home, she read a story to George before he went to bed. Later, she and Sonny sat talking.

'Why don't we take George to the seaside one day in the summer?' she said.

Sonny looked worried again. 'We don't have the money, Maud,' he said. 'Maybe we can take him to the pictures* on Friday instead.'

Maud gave Sonny a small smile, and thought about her words to Mr Lloyd George. Could their lives ever be better? It felt difficult to imagine.

---

* At this time, 'the cinema' was called 'the pictures'.

A few weeks later, news came from Parliament. Prime Minister* Asquith had made a decision on votes for women. Violet and Maud went to the House of Commons. Both pinned suffragette colours of green, purple and white to their coats and hats.

* The Prime Minister is the leader of the government.

When they reached Westminster, they met Edith, and joined a big crowd of women. Everyone was excited, and they sang suffragette songs. It felt like a party, although there were a lot of police watching the crowd.

'There!' Maud said suddenly. 'There he is!'

Mr Lloyd George came out of the Commons. He climbed onto a box and began to speak. The women pushed close together to listen.

'Thank you to all the ladies who came to speak at the House of Commons,' he began. 'The Prime Minister has read all your words. He has spoken to many MPs, especially those who believe in votes for women. He has decided, however, that the time is not right to give votes to women. Thank you.'

As he stepped down, the women's excitement turned to shock and anger. They began to jeer.

Maud couldn't believe it. 'But he listened to us,' she said to Violet. 'They wrote it all down.'

The crowd became noisier and pushed towards Mr Lloyd George, as he tried to get into a waiting car. Police held the women back.

'Liar!' shouted Edith, next to Maud.

'Liar!' Maud shouted along with her.

As Mr Lloyd George's car moved through the crowd, the women banged on the roof and doors. Police officers pulled them back. Other police moved in among them. They began to hit the women, beating them with sticks, and pulling them to the ground.

'Stop it!' cried Maud. 'Leave us alone!'

Edith had blood on her face. A policeman put his arm around her neck and threw her into the back of a van. Violet was next. Even Alice Haughton was attacked.

Maud screamed as a policeman pulled her by the hair and pushed her into the van with the other women.

Inspector Steed stood beside the entrance to the House of Commons, watching. The police had planned this attack, but that didn't mean he liked it.

✲✲✲

The women sat in a line at the police station. Mr Haughton, Alice's husband, soon arrived to collect her.

'How much is it?' he asked the policeman behind the desk.

'Two pounds, sir,' said the officer.

'You must pay for all of us,' said Alice. 'Twelve pounds – there are six of us. Please, Benedict. It's my money!'

Mr Haughton turned and took her arm tightly. 'And you're my wife,' he said. 'You will do what I say, Alice. I've had enough of this.'

And he led her out of the station, leaving the other women behind.

✲✲✲

Maud sat opposite Inspector Steed in the interview room. The clock on the wall showed that it was nearly six.

'I'm late for my son,' she said. 'He needs his dinner.'

'You're not going home for dinner,' the inspector said softly.

Maud was shaking. She hid her hands under the table.

'You're going to prison,' he said.

'I'm not a suffragette,' said Maud.

'I'm glad,' said Inspector Steed. 'You know what the newspapers will say? They'll say that you women listen to your hearts instead of your heads. They'll say you're not sensible enough to vote. I don't agree with them. But it doesn't matter what I think. My job is to keep the law, Mrs

Watts. So I'm going to give you some advice. You'll go to prison. At worst, you'll get a week. Then you'll go home to your husband and forget all this suffragette business.'

The inspector stood up and went to the door.

'They lied to us,' said Maud.

'They didn't lie,' he said. 'They promised nothing and they gave nothing.'

✳✳✳

Holloway prison was cold and grey.

'Dress, one. Coat, one. Boots, one pair,' called out a guard, writing down each piece of clothing as the guards pulled them roughly from the women.

'We are political prisoners,' said Edith, trying to stop them. 'We have the right to wear our own clothes.'

But nobody was listening.

Maud shook with cold as she put on the thin prison dress. A guard took her to her cell, which contained nothing but a hard, metal bed.

She thought about her son waiting for her at home, and started to cry.

'I'm sorry, Georgie,' she whispered. They had never spent a day apart before.

***

Sonny was carrying baskets of washing through the laundry.

'Can't you control that wife of yours?' one of the men said to him.

'What kind of example is she for your George?' said another.

Sonny didn't reply.

Later, he passed Ellyn's, the chemist's. Someone had written 'DIRTY PANKS'* in big red letters on the outside of the shop. Hugh Ellyn was trying to clean it off.

***

The women were allowed to exercise in the prison yard for an hour each day. It was their only chance to talk. Violet and Edith introduced Maud to Emily Davison, another suffragette. Emily had spent more time in prison than any of them. She looked thin and ill, and Violet explained that she was on hunger strike.

'Mrs Pankhurst wants us all to go on hunger strike, like Emily,' Edith told Maud. 'She's refusing to eat until they accept that we are political prisoners.'

'Don't ask Maud to do it,' said Violet. 'It's her first time inside.'

* This meant followers of Emmeline Pankhurst.

A loud whistle blew, and the women began to walk back towards the buildings.

'Faster!' shouted a prison guard. 'Move it!'

***

Six days later, Maud left Holloway prison and hurried home to Bethnal Green. The door key wasn't in its usual place and the house was quiet. When she knocked, the door opened suddenly, and Sonny pulled her inside.

'How's George?' she asked.

'He's asleep,' said Sonny sharply.

'I'm sorry, Sonny,' said Maud. 'I tried to get home, but they kept us there.'

Sonny wasn't interested in Maud's story. 'The police were here,' he said. 'The whole street's whispering about you. I told Taylor that you were sick, but I'm sure he knows the truth ...'

'Mummy,' said a small voice.

'Georgie!' Tears ran down Maud's face as her son ran towards her.

'Back to bed, Georgie,' Sonny said.

Maud kissed George. 'I'll be there in a minute.'

She started to wash up the pile of dirty cups and plates in the kitchen area.

'I waited and waited for you to come home,' said Sonny. His face was red with anger. 'Don't ever do that to me again.'

CHAPTER 6

MRS PANKHURST

'Get your coat and go!' shouted Mr Taylor, pushing Violet towards the door. 'You're nothing but trouble.'

Violet turned and shouted out across the laundry. 'Votes for women!'

Later, Mr Taylor came to speak to Maud. Like Violet, it was her first day back after their week in prison.

'Are you feeling better?' he asked. 'Sonny tells me that you've been unwell.'

Maud looked at him and at Maggie, who was ironing on the other side of the table. Mr Taylor came close to Maud and spoke in her ear.

'It's all right,' he whispered. 'I've got someone else to work extra hours in my office now. You can keep your job if you keep your mouth shut.'

Mr Taylor was speaking to Maud but looking at Maggie. Maggie looked down with tears in her eyes. Maud felt sick.

At the end of the day, Violet was waiting outside for Maud.

'There's a big meeting on Friday evening,' she said quietly. 'They say that Mrs Pankhurst is going to speak. You'll come, won't you?'

'I can't, Violet,' said Maud.

'You have to,' said Violet, but Maud hurried away.

***

That night, Maud lay in bed awake.

'If we have another baby and it's a girl,' she said to

Sonny, 'what will we call her?'

'Margaret,' said Sonny. 'After my mother.'

'And what kind of life will she have?' asked Maud.

'The same as yours,' said Sonny, turning over to go to sleep.

Maud thought of her life, of Maggie's life and of a daughter's life. She made a choice.

'I'm working late tomorrow night, Sonny,' she said.

✶✶✶

It was Friday evening, and Maud was hurrying along a dark street towards Camden Square in north London.

'Come on, Maud!' called Violet, when she saw her. She was waiting with Emily Davison and Edith at the corner of the square. They could hear the sound of excited voices.

'Sorry I'm late,' said Maud.

'Come on,' said Edith. 'We don't want to miss Mrs Pankhurst. She hasn't spoken for months.'

A big cheer went up as a woman appeared at a window on the first floor. It was Emmeline Pankhurst. Mrs Pankhurst opened her arms to calm the women below her. Maud took hold of Violet's arm in excitement.

'My friends,' said Mrs Pankhurst. 'The government does not want me to speak to you, but I am speaking to you anyway!'

More cheers rose into the night sky.

'I know it is difficult for many of you to be here this evening,' she continued. 'I know many of you have left your old lives and your families. For fifty years we have worked to win the vote for women. We have had meetings, we have talked and we have marched. Men have laughed at us. They have refused to listen to us. And they have beaten us. Words are no longer enough. Now, we must act.'

A police car pulled up in a street next to the square and officers climbed out.

'We want every little girl born in this world to have the same chances as her brothers. We do not want to break the law, we want to make the law.'

Suddenly, car headlights lit up the women's faces. Mrs Pankhurst began to speak more quickly, knowing that her time was nearly up.

'Be militant!' she cried. 'Break windows. Attack houses. The government has given us no choice.'

The women began to cheer and stamp their feet.

'I call on the women of Britain to fight back!'

As the police came into the crowd, Violet took Maud's hand and with Edith and Emily, they ran around to the back of the house.

A few moments later, Mrs Pankhurst was led through the front door. A scarf covered her face. Women on either side tried to get her to a waiting car, but the police were closing in. Officers pushed through, beating anyone in their way with sticks.

'I've got her,' said an officer, as he reached through and took Mrs Pankhurst's arm. He pulled the scarf from her face.

'Votes for women!' shouted the woman. She wasn't Mrs Pankhurst.

In the street at the back of the house, Edith and the others helped the real Mrs Pankhurst into a car. Edith quickly introduced Maud to Mrs Pankhurst, who took her hand for a moment.

'Never give up the fight, Maud!' said Mrs Pankhurst, and then she was gone. At that moment, Inspector Steed appeared with some police officers.

'Take these women back to their husbands,' said the inspector darkly. 'They'll know what to do with them.'

✶✶✶

The police van stopped outside Maud's house. Sonny was waiting at the door.

'I'm sorry, Sonny,' she said.

'You're a mother, Maud,' he said. 'You're a wife. My wife. That's what you're meant to be.'

'I'm a person, too,' said Maud.

But Sonny wasn't listening. He had her things by the door. Her clothes, her boots, her bag. He threw them all out into the street.

'Get out!' he shouted. And then he shut the door in her face.

Maud banged on the door with her hands.

'Let me see George!' she shouted. 'Sonny!'

Inside the lights went off and everything went quiet.

CHAPTER 7

MR TAYLOR

Maud followed Violet into St. Barthes' church. It wasn't used as a church anymore, and the Bethnal Green suffragettes met there in secret.

'It ain't* much,' said Violet, 'but it's free. I'll get you clothes from the WSPU.'

Violet saw that Maud was crying. She put her arms around her.

'Don't cry,' she said. 'It's better if you stay strong.'

Maud did her best to smile. Violet was right. This was just the start.

✦✦✦

Inspector Steed placed a photograph of Mrs Pankhurst in the centre of his desk.

'Where are you?' he said. 'What are your plans?'

He took out some other photographs from the evening in Camden Square and arranged them in a line. He picked one up.

'You'll tell me,' he said. The woman in the photo was Maud.

Steed called an officer into the room. 'Get these photographs in the newspapers,' he said.

✦✦✦

Next day, at the laundry, nobody spoke to Maud. As she was heating up her iron, Mr Taylor came over with the morning newspaper. He threw it down in front of her. There was her photograph next to pictures of Edith,

* This means 'isn't' – working-class people at the time said 'ain't'.

Violet, Emily and Mrs Pankhurst. The headline read: 'Mrs Pankhurst and her Militants'.

'It's not a bad picture of you, Maud,' said Mr Taylor, with a horrible smile. 'I think I'll cut it out and put it on my wall.'

Maud didn't reply. The iron in her hand was red hot now.

'I want you to leave, Maud.' He moved his hand up her back and whispered in her ear. 'It's sad, really. After everything I've done for you.'

Maud shook with anger. 'You've done nothing for me,' she said. 'Nothing!'

Maud picked up the hot iron and brought it down hard on her employer's hand.

Mr Taylor's scream stopped all work in the Glass House Laundry.

★★★

The police were called to the laundry, along with Inspector Steed. He took Maud into Mr Taylor's office.

'You can go free, Maud,' he said. 'You can walk out of here. In return, you will help me. All you have to do is give me information.'

Maud looked at the wall. 'You don't know what Taylor's done to me. It started when I was twelve.'

'Do you really think anyone listens to girls like you?' said Inspector Steed. 'They don't. You're nothing in the world. And your Mrs Pankhurst doesn't care about Maud Watts. She's using you. She wants you in her army but she doesn't want to know your story.'

The inspector passed his card across the desk to Maud.

'Call me if you have any information,' he said. 'Anything at all.'

★★★

Back at St. Barthes', Maud was looking at one of George's pictures, her eyes filling with tears. She heard the church door open and the sound of women's voices. Edith, Violet and the other East End suffragettes had arrived for their meeting. Violet had brought Maud a warm winter coat from the WSPU.

'Next time, get Taylor's right hand,' said Violet, with a smile, handing her the coat.

'It was an accident,' Maud said quickly.

'Of course it was.' Violet smiled again.

Edith began the meeting. 'Ladies,' she said, 'our campaign is about to get more militant. If you are unhappy with that, please leave now.'

Nobody moved.

'Good!' said Edith. She laid a large map of London on the table. The postboxes were marked in red and the telephone lines in green. She gave each woman a list of streets.

'Please learn your list and then burn it,' said Edith. 'We'll cut into the heart of the city. We'll start early, before the sun comes up, when the streets are empty. Remember – we must not put anyone's life in danger.'

CHAPTER 8

INSPECTOR STEED

Maud hid on the corner of her old street. Mrs Garston was talking to a neighbour and Maud could see George playing with some other children. She called out to him. As soon as he saw her, his face lit up and he ran over.

Mrs Garston didn't notice as Maud led George away. The two of them went to the park.

'Have you done something very bad, Mummy?' asked George.

'I don't think so, George,' said Maud. 'I just can't come home at the moment.'

'Daddy says you're not well in the head.'

Maud pulled George to her. 'That's not true, George,' she said.

Later, when she took him home, she kissed him three times. 'That's one for today, one for tomorrow, and one to save until I see you next time.'

Sonny appeared at the door and pulled George inside. 'Don't take him again, Maud,' he said.

'George belongs with me, Sonny,' said Maud.

Sonny looked at her coldly. 'The law says he's mine, Maud.'

Maud walked slowly back to the church. She had a lot to think about. Later that evening, she wrote to Inspector Steed.

Dear Mr Steed,

I've thought about your offer and the answer is

no. You see I _am_ a suffragette after all. It's time for

people to listen to girls like me. I've always done

what men told me. But I know better now. I'm

worth the same as you. If it's right for men to fight

to be free, it's right for women too. If the law says I

can't see my son, I will fight to change the law.

Yours,

Maud Watts

Now that she had no job, Maud spent her days at the WSPU offices, answering the telephones and writing letters. In the evenings, she stood outside her old home, waiting to see George at the window. She pulled funny faces and made him laugh until Sonny noticed and took him away.

∗∗∗

The day of Edith's new campaign soon arrived. It was five o'clock in the morning and Maud and Violet were the only people on a street full of houses in the West End. Violet kept watch as Maud walked quickly up to the postbox and dropped a thick letter into it. Both women ran, as a huge bang filled the air and black smoke poured from the postbox.

In a square nearby, there was a second bang, while Edith cycled quickly away from the postbox there.

At the police station in Bethnal Green, Inspector Steed looked at his wall. It had photographs, notes and news stories, all joined with string and pins.

'Another postbox in Cadogan Square,' said an officer,

coming into the room. 'Some telephone lines cut in the Strand. And we got a photo of Miss Withers cutting the lines.'

'Well done,' said Inspector Steed. 'Let's get her.'

★★★

The next day, Maud, Edith and Violet met in the park. Edith was planning the next part of their campaign.

Violet looked worried. 'Miss Withers will get six months in prison at least,' she said. 'I'm not sure I can ...'

'What?' said Edith. 'This is no time to stop. We're in the newspapers. We must make sure that we stay there.'

'The papers just laugh at us,' said Violet.

'They laugh at us because they're afraid of us,' said Edith.

Alice Haughton joined them. She looked around nervously.

'Have you got the information I asked for?' Edith said.

'Yes,' said Alice. 'Lloyd George came to dinner the other evening. The builders haven't finished work on his summer house in Walton-on-the-Hill yet.'

'Perfect,' said Edith. 'Thank you.'

Alice said goodbye and hurried off.

'Her husband won't let her come to meetings any more,' Edith explained to the others.

'Edith,' said Violet. 'This is too much. We can't attack someone's home.'

'The house is empty,' said Edith. 'We won't hurt anyone. Mrs Pankhurst has asked us to be more militant.'

'Then Mrs Pankhurst asks too much,' said Violet angrily, turning and walking quickly across the park.

'Violet!' Maud ran after her. 'What's wrong?'

Violet's eyes were red. 'I'm having another baby,' she

said. 'And I can't even feed the kids I've got.'

'Oh, Violet,' Maud said.

'I'm so tired, Maud,' said Violet. 'I can't go on with all of this. Not now.'

CHAPTER 9

GEORGE

It was George's birthday. Maud knocked on the door of her old home. To her surprise, when Sonny answered the door, he was wearing a suit.

'I just want to say happy birthday.' Maud looked past Sonny, hoping to see George.

'Not now,' said Sonny. He couldn't meet Maud's eyes. 'It's not a good time.'

Maud knew something was wrong. She pushed past him and went inside. A man and woman in coats and hats stood there with George. The woman had her hands on his shoulders.

'Who are you?' said Maud. 'What's happening?'

'This is Mr and Mrs Drayton,' said Sonny. 'They're taking George. He's going to live with them.'

'No,' said Maud.

'We have a very nice home,' said Mrs Drayton. 'With a garden. He'll have everything he needs.'

'NO!' Maud screamed. 'Georgie, come here!'

Mrs Drayton held tightly onto the boy.

'I can't be his mother, Maud,' said Sonny sadly.

'Let me have him,' said Maud.

'We've got no family, Maud. Mrs Garston won't have him. No one round here will take him.'

George ran to his mother and fell into her arms. Sonny looked away, hating himself. Maud took George's birthday present from her pocket and helped him open it. It was a toy animal.

'Listen to me, Georgie,' Maud said, through her tears.

'Your mother's name is Maud Watts. Don't forget that name, George. Come and find me. When you're old enough, will you come and find me?'

Tears ran down George's face. 'Yes, Mummy,' he said.

Sonny pulled George away from Maud and passed him to Mrs Drayton. George started to scream.

'I'm sorry,' said Mrs Drayton to Maud. 'I'll take care of him.'

She picked George up and carried him to the door.

When they had gone, Maud fell to the floor, shaking and crying. Sonny tried to put his arms around her, but she hit him hard around the face.

'What have you done?' she screamed. 'What have you done?'

***

Edith was working in the back room of the chemist's. She was making a bomb.

'Can I help you?' Hugh, her husband, asked.

Edith shook her head. Hugh watched her for a moment.

'Why isn't Violet coming to the meetings any more?' he asked.

'She thinks we're becoming too militant,' Edith said.

'She's not the only one, Edith,' said Hugh. 'Mrs Pankhurst's daughter doesn't agree with the more militant campaign either.'

'We are on the right path,' said Edith.

'And what if you die from one of your bombs?' said Hugh. 'What happens to your campaign then?'

'Then we'll definitely be on the front page of the newspapers!' Edith smiled.

But Hugh wasn't laughing.

***

Hugh stopped the van on a quiet country road near the village of Walton-on-the-Hill. The only light came from the moon. Edith, Maud and Emily Davison jumped out of the back. They walked towards the half-built house. Edith placed her bomb beside one of the walls, and Maud ran a long piece of fuse away from the house. Emily lit the fuse and for a second they watched it burn. Then they ran.

The bomb made a huge bang and the house started to burn. The three women ran as fast as they could back to the van. As Hugh drove away, the women looked back at the burning building, shocked by what they had done.

✷✷✷

The next morning, Maud was walking to the WSPU when she heard her name.

'Mrs Watts?'

Suddenly there were police officers all around her.

'You're under arrest,' one of them said.

They put her in their van and took her to the police station, where Inspector Steed was waiting.

'You women were careful, weren't you?' he said. 'We couldn't find any chemicals on any of you.'

'Then why am I here?' said Maud.

'We'll find something to send you to prison for,' he said.

Maud said nothing.

'My job is to keep the law,' the inspector continued.

'The law means nothing to me,' said Maud. 'I didn't make it. We break windows. We burn things. War is the only language that men listen to.'

'Then we will stop you,' said Inspector Steed.

'What are you going to do?' asked Maud. 'Lock us all up? We're in every home. We're half of all the people in the land. You can't stop us all.'

'Be careful, Mrs Watts,' he said. 'You might lose your life before this is over.'

Maud looked the inspector straight in the eyes. 'But we will win.'

CHAPTER 10

EDITH

Maud sat looking at the walls of her cell in Holloway prison. Every time a meal appeared, she refused to eat it. She was on hunger strike.

On the fifth day, a loud noise outside Maud's cell woke her. Her door banged open and three guards and a doctor came in. They tied Maud's hands and pushed her into a chair.

'Hold her still,' said the doctor. Maud's head was pulled back as he pushed a long tube up her nose. Maud cried out in pain, but the guards held her down.

Inspector Steed stood outside the cell, listening.

As the doctor poured milk through the tube, Maud continued to fight, kicking the bowl of milk against the wall of the cell.

As Maud's cries of pain became louder, the inspector found it too difficult to listen. He left the prison and went straight to the House of Commons. He found Mr Haughton there and told him about what was happening in Holloway.

'These are young women, sir,' said the inspector. 'They're not animals.'

'What else can we do?' said Mr Haughton. 'They won't stop their campaign.'

'They won't break, sir,' said the inspector. 'If one of them dies, we'll have blood on our hands. It will only help their campaign.'

'That must not happen, Inspector,' said Mr Haughton. 'We cannot let Mrs Pankhurst win.'

∗∗∗

A few days later, the door to Holloway prison opened. Maud and Emily helped Edith out into the street. All three women were weak, but Edith seemed very ill. Hugh looked worried as he led her towards the van.

Maud returned alone to the church. She was reading in bed when she heard a voice from the dark.

'Maud?'

It was Violet. 'I brought you some soup and bread,' she said.

'Thanks, Vi.' Grateful, Maud began to eat.

'Not so fast,' said Violet. 'Just a little at a time. Your stomach will hurt after what they did to you.'

Maud put her spoon down for a moment. 'How's Maggie?' she asked.

'She's working long hours at the laundry,' said Violet. 'She's the only one who's earning any money.'

She looked away, tears forming in her eyes.

***

The next day, Maud went to work at the WSPU office. When she arrived, there were papers all over the floor. Edith, Hugh and Emily were tidying up.

'What happened?' asked Maud.

'The police came first thing this morning,' said Emily. 'There were six arrests.'

Maud looked at Edith. She was extremely pale.

'Edith,' she said. 'You're not well. What are you doing here?'

Edith changed the subject. 'There's a meeting outside the House of Commons tonight,' she said. 'Mrs Pankhurst's still on hunger strike, and she may die in prison.'

'The King must free her,' said Emily.

'He's not going to free her,' said Edith.

'Then we must make him,' said Maud.

'How?' asked Edith. 'The government controls the newspapers. There were only a few lines about the bombing of Lloyd George's house! How do we get people's attention?'

'We need the world's attention,' said Emily.

'Then let's go straight to the King,' said Maud.

Hugh looked at Maud. 'Edith can't go to prison again,' he said. 'Her heart isn't strong enough.'

Emily picked up that day's newspaper. 'Look!' she said. 'It's the Derby* at Epsom on Wednesday and one of the King's horses is running ...'

'... and the King will be there!' said Maud.

'They'll stop you at the gates,' said Hugh. 'They'll never let you in.'

'There'll be big crowds,' said Maud. 'Nobody will notice us. We can buy tickets like everyone else.'

Edith's eyes shone. 'We'll wave our flag in front of the world's cameras!' she said.

✦✦✦

A police officer came into Inspector Steed's office.

'We've got some new photos of the women,' he said. 'Here's one of Maud Watts. She's sleeping in St. Barthes' church.'

The inspector looked at the photograph and then picked up his coat.

✦✦✦

Edith had her coat on, ready to go to the Derby. 'Are you ready, Hugh?' she said.

Hugh was finishing some orders before closing the shop.

* The Derby is the biggest horse race in the UK.

'Nearly,' he said. 'I just need some cough mix. Could you get me some from the back?'

'Why didn't you do this last night?' said Edith, putting a suffragette flag into her bag. 'We'll be late.'

'Sorry!'

Edith unlocked the back room and went in.

'What did you want?' she called out. 'Cough mix?' Then she heard the key turn in the lock. 'Hugh! What are you doing?'

She banged on the door. 'Hugh! Let me out!'

Hugh pressed his head against the door. 'I can't, Edith. You've given enough. Your heart is too weak. I'm sorry.'

✳✳✳

Inspector Steed walked quickly into St. Barthes' church. On Maud's bed lay a newspaper. He picked it up. 'Derby Today!' was the headline. He ran for his car.

✳✳✳

Maud watched the passing countryside through the train window. In her hand, she held a ticket to the Epsom races.

There were several entrances to the racecourse, with men checking tickets at each gate. Maud waited in line at one gate, and caught sight of Emily at another. The crowds were pushing forward, wanting to get inside.

Suddenly, Maud felt a hand on her shoulder. She turned and saw a police officer. Her heart stopped.

'Over there, miss. Look!' said the officer. 'There's a shorter line.'

CHAPTER 11

EMILY

People were finding places all around the racetrack where they could watch the horses. Maud looked out across the crowd. She could see the heads of the jockeys in their bright hats as they rode around in a circle.

'There he is!' she said to Emily. 'There's the King!' They could just see him talking to his jockey.

Emily saw a place halfway around the course. 'We can wave our flags from over there,' she said.

There were just a few minutes until the start of the race. People pushed closer together, and it was hard for the two women to get through. Emily took the lead and Maud followed.

Not far away, Inspector Steed was also moving through the crowd, searching for the suffragettes.

The horses were at the start line. A man stood at the side, with a flag in the air, ready to start the race.

Emily finally reached the edge of the course. Across the track were photographers and film cameramen.

The flag was brought down and the race began. Emily could hear the horses coming closer. The crowd cheered, shouting out the names of their favourite horses.

Maud was still a little way behind Emily and called out to her.

Emily turned and smiled for a short moment. 'Never give up the fight, Maud,' she said.

A deep fear filled Maud. As the horses passed, she called Emily's name again. But Emily didn't answer. Unable to stop her, Maud watched as Emily went under the fence and onto the racetrack. As the King's horse came towards her, she ran at it with the suffragette flag.

'Emily!' screamed Maud.

It was over in a second. The horse ran over Emily and then it fell too, throwing the jockey to the ground. Screams filled the air, as the world's cameras caught the moment.

The King was hurried away by his guards, as people ran onto the racecourse to help. The suffragette flag lay on the grass, next to Emily's broken body. Maud ran towards her but she was pushed back as Emily was carried away.

Maud pulled her coat tightly around herself, as tears of shock ran down her face. She was about to leave, when she saw Inspector Steed. Neither of them spoke. Maud didn't care if he arrested her. But the inspector stood to one side and let Maud pass.

✷✷✷

Maud walked through the streets of the East End, back to St. Barthes'. All she could think of was Emily. Would her death make a difference? Had she died for nothing? She passed some children laughing and playing in the street and stopped. Suddenly, she turned around and started running towards the Glass House Laundry.

All the women in the laundry stopped work and watched Maud as she walked straight up to Maggie. Maud took Maggie's hand.

'It's all right, Maggie,' she said. 'You're coming with me.'

'Oi!' shouted Mr Taylor. 'Maud!'

But they had already gone.

After a while, Maud and Maggie came to a street in an expensive part of London. Maud led Maggie up the steps of a large house and knocked on the door.

Alice Haughton appeared.

'Maud?' she said.

'This is Maggie, Violet's daughter,' Maud said quickly. 'She can wash and iron clothes beautifully – she's the best in the laundry. And she can clean.'

Alice understood what was happening and opened the door wider.

'Come in, Maggie,' she said.

Maud gave Maggie a gentle push. 'Be good,' she said.

Alice wanted Maud to come in too. But she was already hurrying away down the street.

***

The next day, when Maud arrived at the WSPU office, Edith was there. She held up a newspaper.

'It's in every paper,' she said. 'They say thousands will be on the streets for Emily's funeral.'

Maud put her arms around Edith. Through her tears, Maud smiled. 'We go on, Edith,' she said. 'You taught me that.'

✱✱✱

On the day of the funeral, the WSPU office was filled with white flowers. Hundreds of women had joined the suffragettes, and Violet and Maggie were laying out teacups on a long table. Maud smiled at Maggie. Outside, crowds of people were lining the streets for the funeral of Emily Wilding Davison.

Maud looked in the mirror and fixed her hat. And then she stepped out into the bright sunshine.

THE END

WHAT HAPPENED NEXT?

Five years later, in 1918, after the end of World War One, the British government gave the vote to women over the age of thirty who owned houses. After another ten years, in 1928, the vote was given to all women over the age of twenty-one.

When did women around the world win the vote?

1893	New Zealand
1902	Australia
1913	Norway
1917	Russia
1918	Austria, Germany, Poland, UK
1920	United States of America
1932	Brazil
1934	Turkey
1944	France
1945	Italy
1949	China, India
1953	Mexico
1971	Switzerland
1974	Jordan
1976	Nigeria
2003	Qatar
2015	Saudi Arabia

The Suffragettes

Women in Britain began campaigning for the right to vote in the 1850s. By 1900, nothing had changed and many women were tired of waiting. One woman, Emmeline Pankhurst, decided to act. She started the Women's Social and Political Union (WSPU) in 1903, and called for action not words.

Emmeline Pankhurst

OF WOMEN WORKERS.
TO FIGHT,
TO STRUGGLE,
TO RIGHT THE WRONG

Buckingham Palace, 1914

Suffragettes in south London, 1911

Taking London by surprise

The suffragettes shocked London from the start. Women chained themselves outside famous buildings.

In 1908, around 300,000 women from all over Britain came to London. They marched through the streets of the capital to a political meeting in Hyde Park. They blew up postboxes and attacked works of art. In 1914 one woman cut through a famous painting of Venus in London's National Gallery with a knife.

The women weren't afraid to go to prison. Over one thousand suffragettes were sent to Holloway prison between 1903 and 1914. Like Maud, many went on hunger strike and were force fed.

Purple, green and white:
the women's movement today
still uses suffragette colours.

More than just the vote

The suffragettes were not just interested in voting.

- They wanted equal pay for women.
- They wanted protection for women.
- They wanted university education to be open to everyone.

Women in Britain today

Of course, women in Britain have the vote today. But they are still not equal.

- In 2015, 25% of women live with violence at home.
- On average, women earn 20% less than men.
- Education is open to all, but it is usually boys who take subjects like physics.
- Although women are 51% of the British people, only 29% of Members of Parliament, 25% of judges and 24% of top business people are women.

Who were the suffragettes?

Women with very different lives joined the suffragettes. But many of the most militant suffragettes were unmarried young women from richer families. They didn't have to work and they didn't have children, so they had less to lose.

War work

When World War One started in 1914, Mrs Pankhurst stopped all militant action, and instead asked women to help their country. The suffragettes had already shown the world what women could do; now they took over men's jobs easily. Between 1914 and 1918, while the men were away fighting, women did men's work. Women's right to vote came at the end of the war.

Discussion:
If the women's movement put bombs in postboxes today, what would we think?

What do these words mean?
You can use a dictionary.
to chain education to force feed
violence on average physics

SELF-STUDY ACTIVITIES

CHAPTERS 1–2

Before you read

You can use your dictionary.

1 Complete the sentences with the correct words.

bell   campaign   class   flag   iron   laundry   slogan

a) You shout or write a … to share your message with other people.
b) You use a hot … to make clothes flat.
c) You take clothes to a … if you don't have a washing machine.
d) In many schools, a … rings at the end of every class.
e) Every country has its own … .
f) In the past, working … people left school at a young age.
g) You run a … to try to change things.

2 Choose the best words in *italics* to complete the sentences.

a) The campaign was very *shocked / militant* and many people died.
b) People were *militant / shocked* when they read about the attacks.
c) The footballer tried to *jeer / control* the ball and shoot at the goal.
d) The crowd *controlled / jeered* when the footballer fell over.

3 Look at pages 4–7. Answer these questions.

a) Who doesn't work at the laundry?
Maud   Edith   Violet   Sonny
b) Who isn't a suffragette?
Violet   Emmeline Pankhurst   Emily   Maud
c) Why didn't the campaign before 1900 win the vote for women?
d) In what way was Mrs Pankhurst's new campaign different?

After you read

4 Answer these questions.

a) Who is Maud looking forward to seeing after work?
b) Who usually takes clean laundry back to its owners?
c) Who does Maud see among the women throwing stones?
d) How does Sonny describe the suffragettes?
e) How does Maud help Violet the next day?
f) Who is Mrs Haughton looking for outside the factory?
g) What does Maud think about breaking windows?

Before you read

5   Complete the text with the words below.

   arrested   bang   bomb   cell   chemicals   coins   hunger strike

   A criminal made a **(a)** ... with dangerous **(b)** .... There was a loud
   (c) ... as he blew open the big metal door of a bank. As he ran out
   of the bank, some **(d)** ... fell out of his pocket. The police found his
   fingerprints on them, and **(e)** ... him the next day. 'I'm not guilty,'
   the man said. 'You haven't got enough proof.' He went on **(f)** ... to
   protest and didn't leave his **(g)** ... for a week.

After you read

6   Are these sentences true or false?

   a) Sonny earns more than Maud.
   b) Edith Ellyn doesn't want anyone to know that she's a suffragette.
   c) Secret cameras take photos of women going into the suffragette
       meeting.
   d) Violet's husband believes in votes for women.
   e) Maud was planning to go to the suffragette meeting at Ellyn's.
   f) Maud has had trouble from Mr Taylor since she was Maggie's age.
   g) Sonny doesn't want Maud to draw attention to herself.

7   Answer the questions.

   a) Why can't Violet speak at the House of Commons?
   b) Why doesn't Maud want to speak?
   c) How did Maud's mother die?
   d) What dangers do the women face at the laundry?
   e) How do the MPs feel while they are listening to Maud?
   f) Who knows more about chemistry – Edith or her husband?
   g) Why can't Sonny and Maud take George to the seaside?

8   Correct the sentences.

   a) The Prime Minister has not read what the women said to the MPs.
   b) The women are happy when they hear Mr Lloyd George's news.
   c) Alice Haughton controls her own money.

d) Inspector Steed doesn't believe women are sensible enough to vote.

e) Edith and Maud share a cell in Holloway prison.

f) Sonny wants to hear about prison life when Maud gets home.

9 What do you think?

How does Maud feel ...

a) when she sits in front of Mr Lloyd George?

b) when she learns that Edith is a scientist?

c) when she learns that Emily Davison is on hunger strike?

CHAPTERS 6–8

Before you read

10 Complete the sentences with the correct verb.

cheer   give up

a) You are at a pop concert. The band start playing. You ... loudly.

b) You are online, trying to buy tickets for your favourite band. After three hours, you ... waiting.

After you read

11 Answer the questions.

a) What lie has Sonny told Mr Taylor?

b) What lie does Maud tell Sonny?

c) What does Mrs Pankhurst want the suffragettes to do?

d) How does Mrs Pankhurst escape the police?

e) What happens when Maud gets home on that Friday evening?

12 Complete these sentences with the correct names.

a) ... helps Maud when she is most alone.

b) ... wants to use Maud as a spy.

c) ... tells Maud that she has lost her job.

d) ... attacks Mr Taylor with a hot iron.

e) Inspector Steed tells Maud that ... is using her.

f) Maud cries because she is missing ... .

g) ... gives the women instructions for more militant actions.

13 Answer the questions.
- **a)** Why can't Maud take George to live with her?
- **b)** What two things do the women do to get the world's attention?
- **c)** Why is Miss Withers going to prison for six months?
- **d)** Why can't Violet continue with the campaign?

CHAPTERS 9–11

Before you read

14 Make sentences.
- **a)** A funeral ...   i) allows you to set off a bomb safely.
- **b)** A jockey ...   ii) takes place after a person dies.
- **c)** A fuse ...   iii) rides a horse in a race.

After you read

15 Answer these questions.
- **a)** Where are Mr and Mrs Drayton taking George?
- **b)** What building do the women blow up?
- **c)** Does Inspector Steed have proof that Maud took part in the bombing?
- **d)** What does the inspector think of the prison doctor making Maud eat?
- **e)** What do the women plan to do at the Epsom Derby?

16 Are these sentences true or false?
- **a)** Emily and Maud travel to Epsom together.
- **b)** Inspector Steed follows the women to Epsom.
- **c)** Maud knows what Emily is going to do as the horses come around the corner.
- **d)** Inspector Steed tries to arrest Maud.
- **e)** Maud rescues Maggie from the Glass House Laundry.

17 What do you think?
Which of the suffragettes in the book had the most difficult choices?

What do these new words mean?

arrest (n & v) ....

bang (n & v) ....

bell (n) ....

bomb (n & v) ....

campaign (n & v) ....

cell (n) ....

cheer (n & v) ....

chemical (n) ....

class (n & adj) working class ....

　　　　middle class ....

coin (n) ....

control (n & v) ....

flag (n) ....

funeral (n) ....

fuse (n) ....

give up (phrasal v) ....

hunger strike (n) ....

iron (n & v) ....

jeer (n & v) ....

jockey (n) ....

laundry (n) ....

militant (adj) ....

shocked (adj) ....

slogan (n) ....

tube (n) ....

whistle (n & v) ....